ART FROM SAND AND EARTH

with projects using clay, plaster and natural fibres

Gillian Chapman & Pam Robson

HODDER
Wayland

Art from Fabric
Art from Packaging
Art from Paper
Art from Rocks and Shells
Art from Sand and Earth
Art from Wood

For more information on this series and other Hodder Wayland titles, go to www.hodderwayland.co.uk

This book was prepared for Wayland (Publishers) Ltd by Globe Education, Nantwich, Cheshire
Artwork and design by Gillian Chapman
Photography by Rupert Horrox

First published in 1996 by Wayland (Publishers) Ltd

This paperback edition published in 2005 by Hodder Wayland, an imprint of Hodder Children's Books

Printed in China

British Library Cataloguing in Publication Data
Chapman, Gillian
Art from Sand and Earth. – (Salvaged series)
I. Title. II. Robson, Pam. III. Series
745.5

ISBN 0 7502 4785 1

Picture Acknowledgments
Life File 4 (Emma Lee), 5t (Nicola Sutton), 5b (Sue Davies)

Hodder Children's Books
A division of Hodder Headline Limited
338 Euston Road, London NW1 3BH

Contents

Resources from Earth

Earth's Resources

People have always used the Earth's natural resources to make things to suit their needs. In the beginning easily-found resources were used to make basic necessities such as food, shelter and clothing. Today, technology has advanced to such a level that even the most inaccessible natural resources can be taken from the Earth and used to manufacture materials for our use. In the manufacture of these materials, vast amounts of energy are consumed, and cannot be replaced. Using natural, renewable materials avoids this energy wastage.

Traditional Pottery Vase from Morocco in North Africa

History and Technology

Technology advances when people discover new ways of using materials. The earliest civilizations learned that clay could be moulded to make pots. The first bricks were shaped thousands of years ago when clay combined with straw was discovered to be a good building material. By 2500 BC the Bronze Age had begun.

People had realized that copper and tin could be combined to make bronze. The Iron Age began with the smelting of iron from iron-bearing rocks. Alloys like steel appeared in the nineteenth century. The twentieth century may perhaps be remembered as the Plastic Age – plastic is a material that creates massive recycling problems.

Out of the Earth

Most people feel the need to have beautiful things around them. The earliest examples of art and craft were created from Earth's rocks, minerals and soils. Sculptures were carved, clay was moulded. The first artists took all their raw materials from the Earth – dyes, sands and clays. Artists' tools were made by shaping available natural objects like flint. The Navajo Indians relied upon the magic of their sand paintings to dispel evil and cure ills. Cave paintings can still be seen today. A belief in powerful spirits of the natural world inspired this traditional art. Wall paintings of traditional homes in northern Ghana are created with paints made from earth pigments.

Aboriginal rock paintings at Ubirri Rock, Kakadu, Australia.

In Zimbabwe, Africa, village women weave baskets from natural fibres.

On the Earth

The Earth also supports a thriving ecosystem of animals and plants. Many provided the first raw materials used by artists. Fibres, fleece and hair were spun, dyed and woven. Found objects were often a source of inspiration. Wood was carved and chiselled, while bark provided a good surface to paint on. Aboriginal Dreamtime art was created with sticks and natural pigments.

Saving the Earth

By using renewable natural materials taken directly from the Earth for art and craft projects, you can make a positive contribution towards the conservation of the Earth's resources.

Sand Painting

Seashore Sands

Seashore sands are found in a range of shades, from black to white. Old lava flows produce black sands; shells and skeletons of marine life produce white sands. On Tahiti the leeward beaches are dazzlingly white, while those on the windward coast are black. The texture of seashore materials also varies greatly from fine-grained sands to huge cobbles like those found on Alaskan beaches.

Desert Sands

Desert sands too can vary in colour and texture depending on the type of rock from which they are formed. Quartz is the most common mineral found in sand. It comes from granite, a rock found worldwide.

Navajo Sand Art

The ceremonial sand paintings created by Navajo spiritual leaders were believed to help restore the balance of life. A sand painting would be created to cure a sick child. The child sat in the centre while the coloured sands, mixed with charcoal and other materials, trickled through the fingers of the healer, forming a painting on the ground. After the ritual the painting was erased.

Coloured Sand Jars

It is very simple to colour sand. Use clean, fine sand. First sieve it to remove any large pieces of grit and shell. Carefully mix the sand with powder paint to make a range of different coloured sands. Spoon layers of sand into clear glass jars. Practise making patterns in the sand by pushing a length of wire or a flexible plastic stick between the sand and the glass. If you put a layer of soil on top of the sand then you can grow small cactus plants in the sand jars.

Coloured Sand Jars

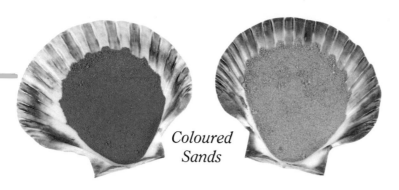

Coloured Sands

Mandala Design

Sand Mandalas

Mandala is the Sanskrit for 'circle'. Mandalas are created by Tibetan monks and coloured sands are used for special occasions. Traditionally, the sands are made from precious stones. The Buddhist mandala is held to be a store of tremendous spiritual energy.

The circular pattern is first drawn in white ink. Then, beginning in the centre, streams of coloured sands are poured through metal funnels. The mandalas are also temporary works of art. After their ceremonial use they are dismantled and dispersed into flowing water, representing the temporary nature of life.

Making a Sand Mandala

Sketch out a circular pattern on card. Carefully paste PVA glue over the areas of the design that will be covered with the same coloured sand. Make a paper funnel and slowly trickle coloured sand on to the glue. Allow the glue to dry and brush away any surplus sand before continuing. Use one colour at a time, filling in the pattern, until the sand mandala is complete.

Colouring the Mandala with the Sand

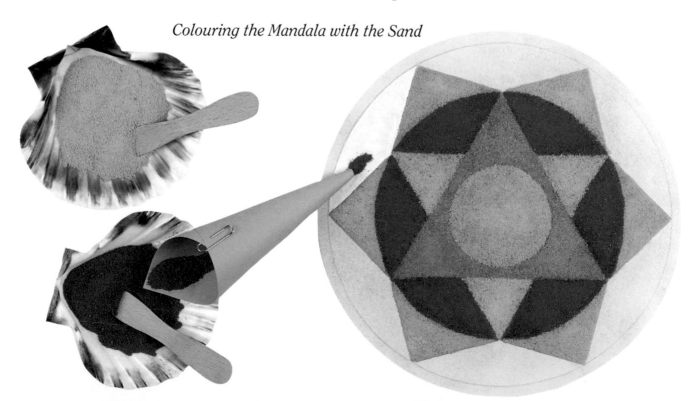

7

Sand Casting

Grains of Sand

Sand forms from eroded fragments of rock. It consists of various minerals and grains of quartz, and is sometimes described as powdered silica. The grains are between 0·06 millimetres and 2 millimetres across. Grains of silt, or mud, are smaller than this; larger grains are known as gravel.

Sand Art

Dry grains of sand will flow through your fingers like water. Have you ever watched sand flow gently downwards through a sand timer? Sand is insoluble in water. When it becomes wet, it can be shaped and moulded. Building sandcastles at the seaside is a popular holiday pastime for grown-ups and children alike.

Sand Moulds

Because wet sand holds its shape you can use it to make moulds. Choose simple shapes, such as the large shells and starfish shown here. Press them into a tray of damp sand to make the mould. Mix up a quantity of plaster, following the instructions on the packet. Carefully pour the plaster into the sand mould using a spoon. Leave the plaster to set hard. Then remove the shape, brushing away any loose sand with a stiff brush.

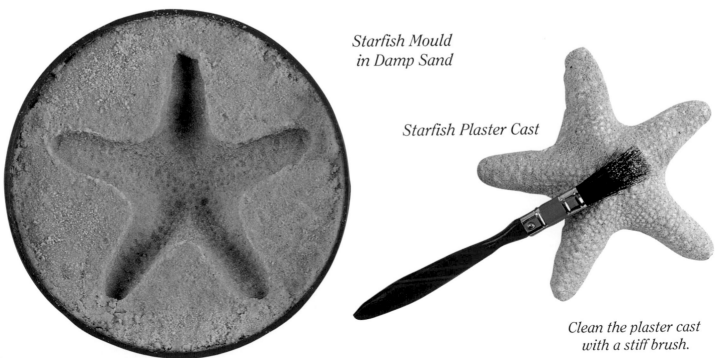

*Starfish Mould
in Damp Sand*

Starfish Plaster Cast

*Clean the plaster cast
with a stiff brush.*

Ripple Patterns in a Tray of Damp Sand

Patterns in Sand

As the sea washes over a sandy shore, moving in and out twice a day with the tides, rippled patterns are left behind in the wet sand. Raking patterns in sand around rocks is an art form found in traditional Japanese gardens. Such works of art are temporary by nature because the wind and the rain will eventually make them disappear.

You can make patterns in damp sand and cast them in plaster to make a more permanent piece of sand art. Fill a tray or large bowl with damp sand. Use your fingers or wooden sticks to make abstract patterns in the sand. When you are happy with the design carefully fill it with plaster, as explained opposite, and wait for it to set. Remove the hardened cast from the tray, brush away any loose sand and paint the cast with poster paints.

Painted Plaster Casts

9

Rock Art

Words in Stone

Some of the oldest writing in the world has been preserved because it is carved in stone. Egyptian stelae, which are carved columns of stone, can tell us much about Ancient Egypt. The Rosetta stone was found in 1799, and its Egyptian hieroglyphics were deciphered in 1822. Today Mayan stelae are broken into small sections by robbers aiming to sell them to collectors.

Icelanders scratched runes, another kind of picture writing, on stone. Pictures and inscriptions carved in stone are called petroglyphs. Neolithic hunters tattooed more than 100,000 such markings in the rocks of Parc de Mercantour in the South of France.

Paint soft chalky rocks and make scratch marks in the surface with wooden tools.

A Rock Collection

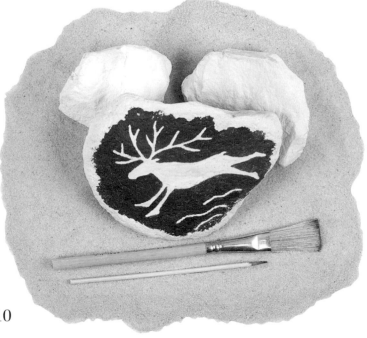

Rock Carvings

Early people often carved on nearby rocks; though carvings on soft rock have been eroded over time. Fine examples of Bronze Age rock carvings of wild animals, ships and sledges can be seen at Tanum, in Norway. Unfortunately the combined effects of tourists' feet and acid rain are wearing away these ancient works of art.

Collect together as many different types of rock as you can find. Try making marks on the surfaces with different tools. Which rocks are easiest to carve?

*Stuffed
Paper Shape*

Rock Paintings

Some of the earliest rock paintings showing human and animal figures have been found in sandstone caves in Queensland, Australia. They are 25,000 years old. The red, yellow and white tints have been made from iron oxides and kaolin pigments.

In the middle of the Sahara desert, on the rocks of the Tassili Plateau, are paintings dating from 5000 BC. At that time, the desert did not exist. Hunting scenes have been painted using pigments ground from the surrounding rocks. Powdered red, yellow, olive and brown ochres and white kaolin were mixed with water, milk or acacia gum.

Making a Rock Painting

Here is a way of making a painting that will look thousands of years old. Find some large sheets of strong paper, or glue sheets of newspaper together to make stronger sheets. Staple two pieces together, around the edge, forming a large paper bag. Stuff the bag with crumpled scrap paper, securing the opening with staples. Paint the surface with a mixture of PVA glue and sand. When dry this will give you a textured 'rock' surface to paint. Look at examples of traditional rock painting in books, then try painting your own.

*Rock
Painting*

11

Mud Prints

Grains of Silt

Like sand, silt or mud is also eroded grains of rock. But silt grains are smaller than sand grains. Silt grains are between 0·004 millimetres and 0·06 millimetres across. Silt is carried by river water. When a river floods, this load of silt is deposited across the valley floor. The land of a flood plain is extremely fertile.

Muddy Shores

Where a large river carrying fresh water enters the sea an estuary is formed. This is known as the mouth of the river. The water is laden with sediment, or silt. Often strong tides and currents carry the silt out to sea or along the shore. If the weight of the silt is heavy enough, it is deposited in the estuary and a delta is formed, like the Mississippi delta.

African Mud Cloths

In parts of west Africa mud is used to create patterns on cloth. The Korhogo of the Ivory Coast and the Bamana of Mali both decorate cloth using a mixture of mud and pigments. Their designs are painted on hand-woven cotton cloth. The mud they use must be specially prepared. It stands, covered with water, in a clay pot for many months.

Making Mud Paints

If you live near to a river estuary, it is the best place to collect mud. However, garden mud will do. Collect enough to fill a large container and mix with water. Filter the mud through a fine mesh strainer to remove any debris. When the mud is 'clean', add some PVA glue to make the paint. Try collecting mud from different places, to make a variety of colours. These can be stored in small containers until ready for use.

Mud paints can be stored in jars.

PVA glue

Add PVA glue to the clean mud and mix thoroughly to make the paint.

Making Mud Paints

Painting on Cloth

You can use mud pigments to paint on to cloth. Use a piece of cotton cloth, from an old sheet, and cut it into a thirty centimetre square. Sketch out your designs first on paper. African artists use simple, bold shapes on their textiles, like the ideas shown here.

Pin the cloth square to a large piece of thick cardboard to hold it taut while you work. Then trace your design on to the cloth. Use the mud pigments to paint in the detail. You may need to add a small amount of water to the mud to make it easier to use.

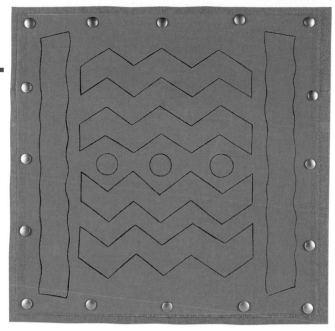

Cloth Stretched on Cardboard

Cloth with Frayed Edge

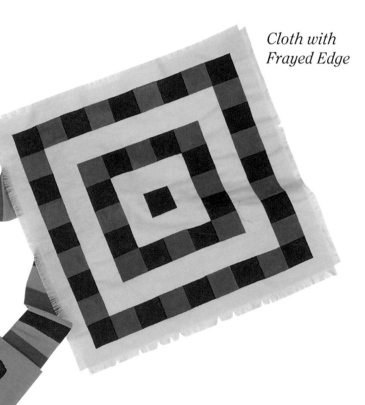

Shoulder Bag

Ideas for Mud Cloths

You may decide to make several painted square cloths. Give them a decorative frayed edge by pulling out the loose threads. Sew two square cloths together to make a cushion cover, or make them into an attractive shoulder bag by adding a shoulder strap.

13

Making Impressions

Clay Soil

Soil is weathered rock. Weathering happens in a number of ways. Extremes of temperature cause expansion and contraction of the rock which then cracks. Water held in cracks may freeze, causing further cracking. Running water can dissolve or erode rock. Plants may grow in cracks, causing erosion. Dead plants help make fertile soil. Clay soil is eroded granite. All clay contains water.

Objects Useful for Making Impressions

Properties of Clay

Clay has plasticity, which means it can be shaped. Primary clays are pure white and are used to make bone china. Secondary clays vary in colour according to the minerals they contain. Pottery is fired clay. It has been heated in a kiln causing an irreversible change.

Clay Tile Impressed with the Objects Above

Clay Artefacts

Since early times clay has been used to make pots. The first bricks were straw mixed with clay. They were used as a building material by the Romans. The domed roof of the Pantheon, built in Rome in AD 120, is made from bricks and concrete. Concrete is a mixture of cement (made from limestone and clay), sand, gravel and water. Today, bricks are made from a mixture of clay and sand.

Clay Tile Decorated with Textured Fabrics

Impressions in Clay

A traditional method of decoration is to beat the clay with a cloth-covered paddle, leaving the imprint of the weave. In north-west Cameroon small carved wooden cylinders are rolled into strips of clay, leaving impressions. The strips are then built into the design of a pot.

Tools to make Impressions

Designs can be impressed into soft clay using a variety of everyday objects. We have used a self-hardening clay that does not need firing. Roll out the clay and make a series of tiles to practise on.

Collect together different plastic and metallic objects, like the ones shown opposite, and use them to make unusual patterns in the clay. Try making impressions using heavily textured fabrics and natural materials such as shells, seeds, fossils and pieces of wood. Dust the objects with talcum powder first to prevent them sticking to the clay.

When you have made a series of patterned tiles, either use them to make plaster casts (see page 12) or leave them to harden. They can then be painted.

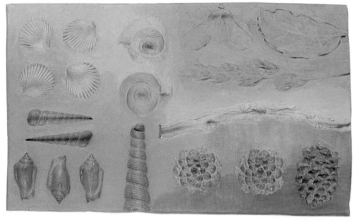

Clay Tile Decorated with Metal Objects

Clay Tile Decorated with Natural Materials

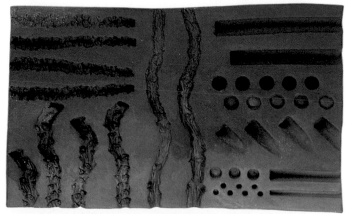

Clay Tile Decorated with Pieces of Wood

15

Patterns in Relief

Gypsum

Gypsum was formed millions of years ago, when dinosaurs roamed the Earth. It is a white rock in which, for each molecule of gypsum there are two molecules of water. It is mined all over the world. Gypsum is turned into plaster by crushing it into a powder. The water is removed by heating.

Alabaster

The Ancient Egyptians and the Romans created beautiful alabaster figures from a special kind of gypsum. The Ancient Egyptians coated the inside walls of their houses with white gypsum or plaster. They then painted the walls with coloured patterns and scenes from nature. Noble Egyptian families had very elaborate wall paintings in their houses. The inside walls of the pyramids were also plastered, and decorated with pictures.

Natural Plaster Collage

Plaster of Paris

Because gypsum was found in the Montmartre district of Paris, it became known as plaster of Paris. When plaster powder is mixed with water it generates heat before hardening. This is because a chemical reaction takes place as the molecules of water react with the gypsum molecules to re-form the original gypsum. The whole process can be reversed by heating and removing the water again.

Making Plaster Collages

A simple way of making a permanent natural collage is to collect together grasses, leaves and natural materials that would normally wither. Arrange and secure them to a strong backing board, such as hardboard. Mix up a thin solution of plaster, following the instructions on the packet, and brush it evenly over the collage. The plant forms will be preserved in the solid plaster.

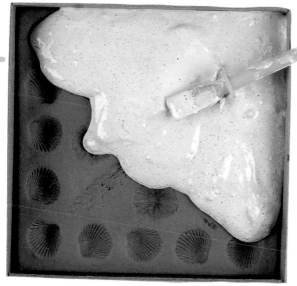

Spreading Plaster over the Mould

Making Plaster Casts

There are examples of impressions in clay on the previous pages. While the clay remains soft you can use impressed tiles as moulds to make plaster reliefs. Place your patterned clay tile on to a flat board. Use pieces of thick card 6 centimetres wide to make a box structure around the tile, as shown here.

Care When Using Plaster

Cover all surfaces with newspaper before you begin. Mix the plaster in old plastic containers, these are easy to clean. Make sure the plaster mixture is free of lumps and bubbles. Work quickly. Never pour unused plaster down a drain.

Mix up some plaster, following the instructions on the packet. Pour a layer of about 3 centimetres evenly on top of the tile and leave to set. Then tear the cardboard sides away and carefully remove the clay mould. Seal the plaster with diluted PVA before painting.

Plaster casts can be painted and varnished.

Plaster Cast of Manufactured Objects

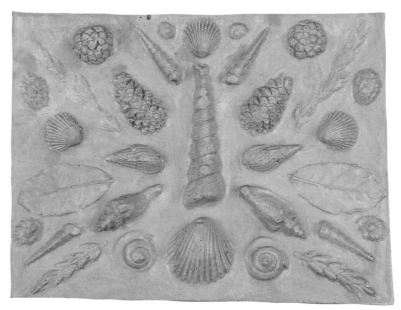

Plaster Cast of Natural Materials

Modelling with Clay

Pottery

Pottery-making is an ancient craft, carried out all over the world. Earth and water are combined by heat to create beautiful and useful artefacts. Archaeologists dig up fragments of pottery from which they can learn much about the past. In museums today we can see fine examples of Ancient Greek pottery decorated with images of daily life and mythology.

The shape and size of pots varies; they are usually made for a particular purpose. The earliest clay pots were shaped from coils of clay; thrown pots made on a wheel came later. Clay, containing traces of iron, turns a lovely shade of red, known as terracotta, when the clay is fired. The words 'terra' and 'cotta' mean 'baked earth'.

Flatten the Base   *Hollow Out the Inside*

Making 'Pebble' Pots

Here is an easy way to shape a clay pot with a lid. Mould a lump of clay in your hands, until it looks like a large, smooth pebble. Flatten one side to be the base, then carefully cut the 'pebble' in half with a sharp cutting tool. The top half will be the lid and the bottom will be the pot. Hollow the pieces, leaving the sides about 1 centimetre thick.

Make textured patterns on the surfaces, or smooth out any unwanted marks with a damp sponge. Check that the lid still fits the pot. Leave to harden completely before painting with powder paints mixed with varnish.

Pebble Pots

18

Clay Whistles

The clay whistle is a traditional Central American wind instrument. Some have one mouthpiece opening, making only one note possible. The Chilean ocarina has finger holes for playing scales.

Making a Bird Whistle

Take a lump of clay and mould it into a bird shape. Then cut the shape in half. Hollow out the two pieces and join them together using a clay and water solution. Use a piece of 1-centimetre wide dowel to make the blow-hole in the tail. Keep the dowel in place while the clay hardens, turning it gently to prevent it sticking. Make three small note holes on one side of the body.

When the clay is hard, cut out the whistle hole with a knife. Cut a 4 centimetre length from the piece of dowel to plug the blow-hole. The whistle noise is made by shaving the plug slightly so air can blow through. You will need to adjust the plug and position it correctly in the blow-hole. When you make a strong note, glue the plug into place. Finally paint and varnish the bird whistle.

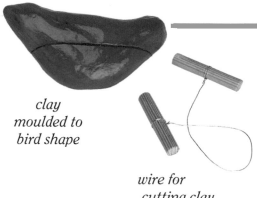

wooden dowel for plug

clay moulded to bird shape

wire for cutting clay

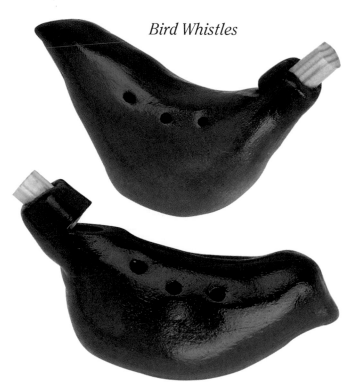

Bird Whistles

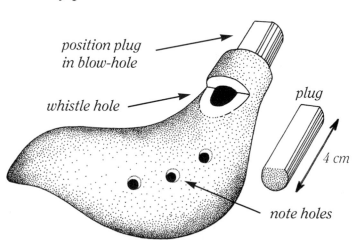

position plug in blow-hole

whistle hole

plug

4 cm

note holes

Working with Self-Hardening Clay

We have used self-hardening clay to make these projects. The clay is easy to obtain in small quantities and does not need to be fired in a kiln. It contains a hardener and will set in a few days. When working on a project, keep the clay moist between sessions by wrapping the model in plastic film or a damp rag. Pieces of scrap wood, wire, plastic and old kitchen utensils make ideal tools for clay modelling.

Plaster Carving

Symbolic Carvings

From the time that the first tools were made, craftspeople have felt the need to carve beautiful shapes. Wood, stone, plaster and jade all lend themselves to this creative technique. Often such carvings were symbolic or religious. The elephant-headed Indian god, Ganesh, is often seen in sandalwood carvings. Vietnamese woodcarvers make figures that represent, happiness or wealth, to give as special gifts.

Tools and Materials

The colour and character of the finished carving reflects the choice of material. The tools used will also be determined by the nature of the material. Wood can be cut, chiselled or chopped, according to its type. Stone can be flaked, chipped or pecked, depending upon its properties. Jade is difficult to carve because of its hardness.

Making a Plaster Block in a Cardboard Mould

Plaster Carving

Plaster is an ideal material to experiment with. It is inexpensive and readily available. Being soft, it easy to carve and shape with a few basic tools. Sketch out your ideas first, drawing simple, solid shapes. You will be working in three dimensions, so think about the size and scale of your carving.

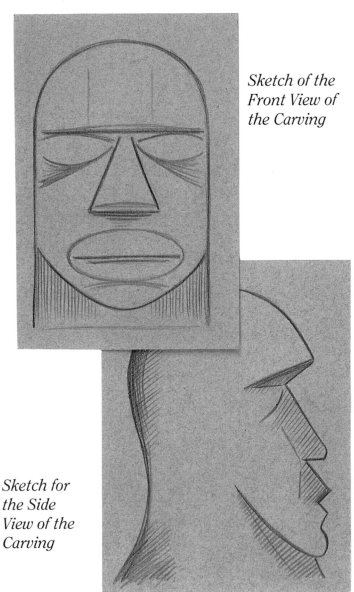

Sketch of the Front View of the Carving

Sketch for the Side View of the Carving

Carving Tools

*Carving Sketched
on to Plaster Block*

Making a Plaster Block

Make a cardboard mould large enough to cast the plaster block. You may even find a suitable plastic container to use. Mix up a quantity of plaster following the instructions on the packet. Pour it carefully into the mould and leave to set hard. Tear off the cardboard, and let the block harden completely before starting to carve.

Preparing to Carve

Refer to your sketches and draw the shape of your carving on to each side of the plaster block. This will be a rough guide when you begin to carve. Place your sketches in front of you and keep referring to them as you work.

Using Tools

Ask an adult if you can use old carpentry tools or kitchen utensils, but use them with care. Carve large areas of plaster away with a rasp, knife or chisel. As the carving takes shape, use smaller tools to cut out details, and smooth the surface with sandpaper. Seal the plaster with PVA glue before painting and varnishing.

*Finished
Carvings*

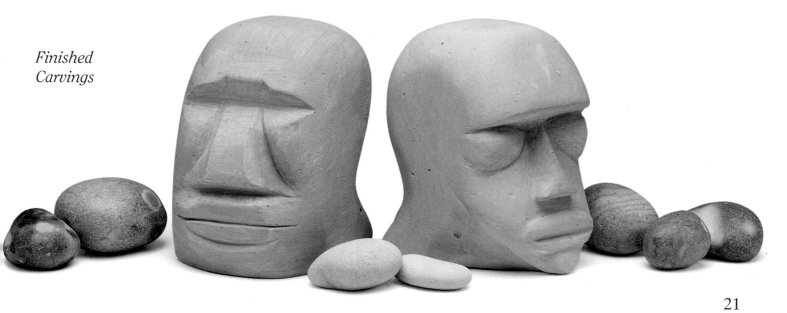

Natural Dyes

Symbolism and Colour

Colour in clothing has always been important, showing age, social position or power. The use of colour has different meanings in different countries. In Europe and America black means sadness, but in China white is the colour of mourning.

Natural Dyes

Minerals and plants were once the main sources of natural dyes. More unusual examples came from insects and molluscs. Purple was made from a rare Mediterranean species of whelk – it became a symbol of high position in the city of Rome. Insects like the South American cochineal beetle produce a range of red colours.

Vegetable Dyes Found in the Kitchen

Vegetable Dyes Found in the Garden

Vegetable Dyes

Dyes can be obtained from roots, bark, berries, grasses and leaves. Traditionally, plants that gave strong colours were highly regarded. Indigo and woad for blue, and madder for red are among the oldest plant dyes known. A bright golden yellow comes from the stigmas of the saffron crocus.

Experimenting with Vegetable Dyes

You can carry out dyeing experiments using common plant materials found in the kitchen and garden. Flowers, leaves and berries should be collected fresh. Tougher materials like bark, fir cones and walnut shells will need to be chopped up and soaked in water overnight. Marigold and dahlia petals give yellows and browns, onion skins dye orange. Try tea, coffee, turmeric or carrot tops.

Dyeing Equipment

Basic Equipment

For these simple experiments gather together as many different dye stuffs as possible. These will have to be chopped up and boiled in water. Use an old stainless steel or enamel saucepan if possible and discarded utensils. You may need the help of an adult with these preparations. Try dyeing scraps of white yarn or pieces of fleece and find out how many shades of colour you can create. A rusty nail or piece of copper wire added to the dye bath will make the colours darker.

Recording Experiments

It is important to keep a record of all your dyeing experiments. While you are working make notes of when and where you collect the dye stuffs and how you prepared them. Make a loose-leaf record book and write up your results. Sketch or photograph the different plants and include samples of the dyed materials.

Dyeing Record Book

Onion skins

1. 1. Brown skins soaked overnight. Boiled & strained. Wool added to liquid and simmered for ½ hour

2. 2. Copper wire added to dyebath.

3. Turmeric Powder

25 gm. turmeric added to water and heated gently.

4. Wool added & simmered for ¼ hour.

4. Copper wire added.

Marigold petals — boiled in water. Wool added and simmered for ½ hour.

Earth's Pigments

Pigments and Paints

A pigment is a colouring agent. Paint is made from a solid pigment mixed with a fluid. Unlike dyes, which dissolve, pigments remain suspended in the fluid.

Paint is a coloured substance which can be applied to a surface. The tools used to apply paint will vary with the nature of the paint. Oil paints are made by mixing pigments with linseed oil. Water-colours are a mixture of pigment and a water-soluble binder.

Colour Wheel (below) Made From the Natural Materials (shown above right)

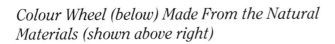

The Earliest Pigments

Clays, rocks and metal ores provided the first pigments. In order to use them for painting, they were mixed with animal fats, gum arabic, beeswax, gelatine or egg whites. The mineral, lapiz lazuli, gave ultramarine blue. The Egyptians crushed minerals like azurite, malachite, and cinnabar to obtain, respectively, blue, green and vermilion red.

Natural Colour Wheel

All the colours of the spectrum occur in nature. Climate and the changing seasons both have an effect on the colour of plants. Make a collection of brightly coloured natural materials, like feathers, minerals, shells, flowers, fruits and vegetables, and arrange them into a natural colour wheel.

marigold   *geranium*

green leaves   *cornflower*

Natural Paints

Making Natural Colours

Medieval artists extracted pigments from flowers, berries and leaves. A bright blue ink was made by crushing cornflower petals and mixing them with water. Oak galls were ground into paste and diluted to make black ink.

Experiment with the plants and fruits in your collection and make some water-colour paints. Flower petals, leaves and berries can be mixed with a small amount of warm water. Squeeze the mixture through a strainer and use the coloured juice like paint.

Earth Painting

Blow drops of paint with a drinking straw to make this tree landscape.

Earth Painting

Water-colours made from flowers and berries are fun to experiment with, but the colours are very pale and will quickly fade. Colours made from earth pigments are also easy to make and are much more permanent, as shown by the existence of cave paintings.

Earth with a high clay content makes the best paint. Collect samples of different coloured earths, also try using chalk and sand to get a range of colours. First sieve out any lumps and grit, then mix the earth with PVA glue. The glue acts as a binder and makes the earth into a paint. The paints can be applied thickly or diluted with water. Use them to paint an earth painting.

Earth Paints

Using Fibres

Sisal

Sisal is a fibrous plant which grew originally only in Central and South America. In the nineteenth century, it was introduced to East Africa where the leaves were used to obtain a strong fibre. In Kenya, it is twined into kiondo bags which are traditional round baskets. In Swaziland, it is used to make colourful coiled baskets.

Jute

The jute plant grows up to 4 metres tall. The fibres are taken from the stem by soaking in water. They are much softer fibres than those obtained from sisal. About 70 per cent of the world's jute is grown in Bangladesh. It was used to provide the raw material for rope, hessian, carpet backing and sacking but since the 1950s, synthetic fibres have gradually been introduced.

Different Strings and Ropes Made From Natural Fibres

Hemp and Flax

It has been suggested that farmland could be planted with fibre crops for use in industry. Machines are being developed which can extract tough stem fibres from such plants, on an industrial scale. Machines have already extracted fibres from hemp, flax and even stinging nettles. Clothing can be woven from these fibres.

During the First World War (1914–1918), the Germans used nettle fibres to make a fabric similar to cotton. Even the waste from the process can be put to use. These woody granules, known as 'shiv', can be turned into animal bedding. Most importantly hemp and flax fibres form a pulp from which paper can be made. They can also be added to recycled paper to restore its strength.

Useful Objects Made From Natural Fibres

Using Fibres

Different fibres are used to make rope and string for different purposes. Around the house and garden, rope and string have many uses. Coarse, strong rope is useful outdoors; fine string will tie up a parcel. See how many thicknesses and types of string you can find.

Coiling the String around a Plastic Container

Making String Bowls

Use scraps of string and rope from your collection to make a string bowl. Find a plastic container or plant pot to use as a mould. Brush PVA glue on to the outside, starting at the base and covering to a depth of 5 centimetres. Begin winding lengths of string around the container.

Continue glueing and winding the string, working around the outside of the container until it is completely covered. It may help to hold the string temporarily in place with masking tape. This can be removed when the PVA dries and the wound string is firmly glued in place. Paint and varnish the finished bowls and use them as plant pots.

Coiled String Bowls

Straw Work

Harvest Time

All over the world superstitious people once believed that gods and goddesses were responsible for the harvest each year. In India the corn spirit was Indra, the thunder god. He was thought to be responsible for the rice harvest. In Egypt the story of Osiris was told. The Romans worshipped Ceres, the goddess of the harvest, from which has come the word 'cereal'.

Corn Figures

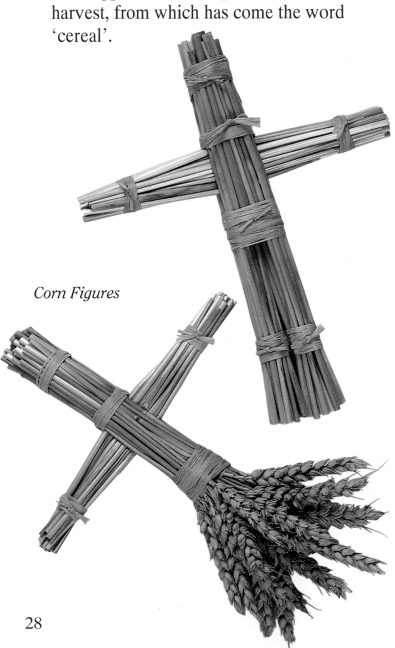

Harvest Emblems

In India today, designs in straw are made with rice straw. They are hung in doorways as good luck charms when young couples marry. The designs are usually in the shape of everyday objects like combs. Sometimes a ram's horn shape is made.

In Britain, corn dollies were once harvest emblems made as offerings of thanks to the gods, or idols, for the crops. It is from 'idol' that the word dolly comes. Native Americans once used corn husks for weaving cloth or wrapping food. When corn husks have been softened in glycerine and water they can also be used to shape doll figures.

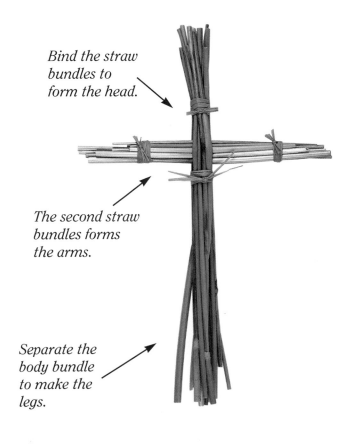

Bind the straw bundles to form the head.

The second straw bundles forms the arms.

Separate the body bundle to make the legs.

Making Corn Figures

By binding lengths of straw together with raffia, you can make a family of corn figures. Start by making small bundles, trimming the straw and tying it with raffia or thread. Make up the figures as shown here. A larger bundle forms the body, with a thinner piece shaping the arms. Try making animal figures in the same way.

Making a Scarecrow

The scarecrow is made in a similar way to the corn figures, but on a larger scale. You will need a quantity of straw, or thin twigs and branches could also be used, if available. A large bundle of straw forms the main body structure, with smaller, thinner shapes for the arms and legs.

Bind the body together with raffia or string. You can then dress the scarecrow in old clothes, and stand it in the vegetable garden.

Natural Materials

Scarecrow

Glossary

alabaster A variety of gypsum which is usually white in colour.

cobbles Large, naturally rounded stones found on certain seashores. Not the same as the cobbles used in road building.

dyes Substances used to stain or colour.

elements Substances that make up the universe. Scientists know of more than 105 elements, each of which contains only one kind of atom.

estuary The part of a river mouth where sea and river water meet and mix.

fabric A cloth made by weaving, knitting or felting yarn or fibres.

fibres Natural or synthetic filaments that can be spun into yarn.

gypsum A mineral of hydrated calcium sulphate found in sedimentary rocks. Used to make plaster.

hieroglyphics An ancient form of writing used in Ancient Egypt in which pictures or symbols represent objects, ideas and sounds.

iron oxides Seen as rust on the surface of iron where the iron has reacted with water and oxygen.

kaolin A fine white clay used to make bone china and porcelain – also known as china clay.

lava Hot magma that flows from an erupting volcano. Igneous rock is solidified lava.

molecule A molecule is the simplest unit of a chemical compound and is formed when two or more atoms combine chemically.

mollusc An invertebrate with a soft, unsegmented body and often a shell. Gastropods, cephalopods and bivalves are all molluscs.

ochres Various natural earths containing ferric oxide, silica and alumina used as yellow and red pigments.

petroglyphs Pictures and inscriptions carved in stone.

pigments Substances found in plant or animal tissue that produce a characteristic colour.

plaster of Paris A white powder that sets hard when mixed with water because a chemical reaction occurs. It is so-called because it was found in the Montmartre district of Paris.

raffia A fibre obtained from the stalks of certain palm trees and used for weaving.

runes Writing symbols from an ancient Germanic alphabet used in Scandinavia up to and during the Middle Ages.

terracotta Unglazed clay or earthenware pottery that is reddish-brown in colour.

More Information

Books to Read

Allen J. & Brown M., *The Last Green Book on Earth*, Red Fox, 1994

Carlson L., *Ecoart!*, Williamson Publishing, 1992

Dean J., *The Craft of Natural Dyeing*, Search Press, 1995

Petrash C., *Earthwise*, Floris Books, 1992

Rescue Mission Planet Earth, Kingfisher, 1994

World Crafts, Merlion Arts Library, 1993

Addresses for Information

Australia

Australian Conservation Foundation, Floor 1, 60 Leicester Street, Carlton, Vic 3053

Canada

International Council for Local Environmental Initiatives, City Hall, East Tower, 8th Floor, Toronto, Ontario M5H 2N2

UK

Ashill Colour Studios, Boundary Cottage, 172 Clifton Road, Shefford, Bedfordshire SG17 5AH

BerryCraft Supplies, Acadia, Swansbrook Lane, Horam, Heathfield, East Sussex TN21 0LD

Centre for Alternative Technology, Machynlleth, Powys SY20 9AZ

Fibrecrafts, Old Portsmouth Road, Peasmarsh, Guildford, Surrey, GU3 1LZ

Places to Visit (UK)

British Museum, Great Russell Street, London WC1B 3DG

Chiltern Open Air Museum, Newland Park, Gorelands Lane, Chalfont St Giles, Buckinghamshire HP8 4AB

Commonwealth Institute, Kensington High Street, London W8 6NQ

Museum of Mankind, Burlington Gardens, London W1X 2EX

Natural History Museum, Cromwell Road, London SW7 5BD

The Colour Museum, 82 Grattan Road, Bradford BD1 2JB

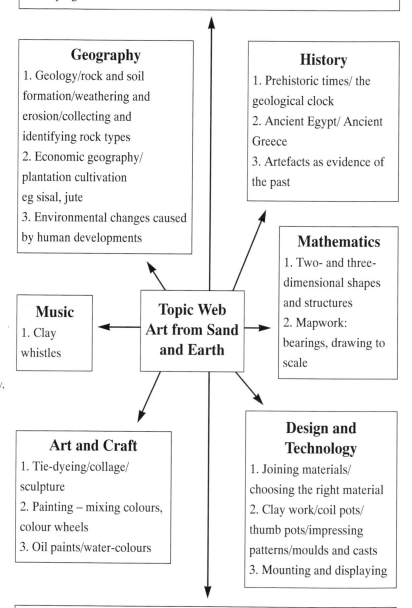

Language and Literature
1. Folk tales and mythology
2. Communication/origins of writing/cave art/runes/hieroglyphs/ clay tablet and stylus/writing tools
3. Keeping records

Geography
1. Geology/rock and soil formation/weathering and erosion/collecting and identifying rock types
2. Economic geography/ plantation cultivation eg sisal, jute
3. Environmental changes caused by human developments

History
1. Prehistoric times/ the geological clock
2. Ancient Egypt/ Ancient Greece
3. Artefacts as evidence of the past

Mathematics
1. Two- and three-dimensional shapes and structures
2. Mapwork: bearings, drawing to scale

Music
1. Clay whistles

Topic Web Art from Sand and Earth

Art and Craft
1. Tie-dyeing/collage/ sculpture
2. Painting – mixing colours, colour wheels
3. Oil paints/water-colours

Design and Technology
1. Joining materials/ choosing the right material
2. Clay work/coil pots/ thumb pots/impressing patterns/moulds and casts
3. Mounting and displaying

Science
1. Light/colour/pigments/dyes
2. Properties of materials/ making new materials/ chemical changes/ reversible/irreversible changes
3. Classification of plants and animals/ecosystems

Index